THIS CRUISE JOURNAL belongs to:

_____

Dedication

This Cruise Journal is dedicated to all the people out there who love to go on a cruise ship and document their findings in the process.

You are my inspiration for producing books and I'm honored to be a part of keeping all of your Cruise notes and records organized.

This journal notebook will help you record your details about tracking your wonderful cruise memories.

Thoughtfully put together with these sections to record:
Date, At Sea or At Port, Weather & Temperature, Meals, Shipboard Activities, Excursions, Evening Events & Attire, Favorite Memory, New Friends, and Notes.

How to Use this Book

The purpose of this book is to keep all of your Cruise ship notes all in one place. It will help keep you organized.

This Cruise Journal will allow you to accurately document every detail about your wonderful trip. It's a great way to chart your course through a magical cruise vacation.

Here are examples of the prompts for you to fill in and write about your experience in this book:

1. Date, At Sea or Port
2. Weather & Temperature
3. Meals - Restaurant & Meals For Breakfast, Lunch Dinner
4. Shipboard Activities
5. Excursions
6. Evening Events & Attire
7. Favorite Memory
8. New Friends
9. Don't Forget - Blank Lined For Notes & Writing Important Information Or Thoughts

Date _____

At Sea ○   Port ○   _____

Weather ☀ ☁ ☂ ❄   Temperature _____

	Restaurant	Menu Choice
Breakfast		
Lunch		
Dinner		

Shipboard Activities

Excursions

Evening events _____

Attire _____

Favorite Memory _____

New Friends _____

Don't forget! _____

Date _____

At Sea ○   Port ○   _____

Weather ☀ ☁ ☂ ❄   Temperature _____

	Restaurant	Menu Choice
Breakfast		
Lunch		
Dinner		

Shipboard Activities

Excursions

Evening events _____

Attire _____

Favorite Memory _____

New Friends _____

Don't forget! _____

Date _____

At Sea ○ Port ○ _____

Weather ☀ ☁ ☂ ❄   Temperature _____

	Restaurant	Menu Choice
Breakfast		
Lunch		
Dinner		

Shipboard Activities

Excursions

Evening events _____

Attire _____

Favorite Memory _____

New Friends _____

Don't forget! _____

Date _____

At Sea ○   Port ○   _____

Weather ☀ ☁ ☂ ❄   Temperature _____

	Restaurant	Menu Choice
Breakfast		
Lunch		
Dinner		

Shipboard Activities

Excursions

Evening events _____

Attire _____

Favorite Memory _____

New Friends _____

Don't forget! _____

Date _____

At Sea ○   Port ○   _____

Weather ☀ ☁ ☂ ❄   Temperature _____

	Restaurant	Menu Choice
Breakfast		
Lunch		
Dinner		

Shipboard Activities

Excursions

Evening events _____

Attire _____

Favorite Memory _____

New Friends _____

Don't forget! _____

Date _____

At Sea ○   Port ○   _____

Weather ☀ ☁ ☂ ❄   Temperature _____

	Restaurant	Menu Choice
Breakfast		
Lunch		
Dinner		

Shipboard Activities

Excursions

Evening events _____

Attire _____

Favorite Memory _____

New Friends _____

Don't forget! _____

Date _____

At Sea ○   Port ○   _____

Weather ☀ ☁ ☂ ❄   Temperature _____

	Restaurant	Menu Choice
Breakfast		
Lunch		
Dinner		

Shipboard Activities

Excursions

Evening events _____

Attire _____

Favorite Memory _____

New Friends _____

Don't forget! _____

Date _____

At Sea ○   Port ○   _____

Weather ☀ ☁ ☂ ❄   Temperature _____

	Restaurant	Menu Choice
Breakfast		
Lunch		
Dinner		

Shipboard Activities   Excursions

Evening events _____

Attire _____

Favorite Memory _____

New Friends _____

Don't forget! _____

Date _____

At Sea ○   Port ○   _____

Weather ☀ ☁ ☂ ❄   Temperature _____

	Restaurant	Menu Choice
Breakfast		
Lunch		
Dinner		

Shipboard Activities

Excursions

Evening events _____

Attire _____

Favorite Memory _____

New Friends _____

Don't forget! _____

Date _____

At Sea ○ Port ○ _____

Weather ☀ ☁ ☂ ❄   Temperature _____

	Restaurant	Menu Choice
Breakfast		
Lunch		
Dinner		

Shipboard Activities

Excursions

Evening events _____

Attire _____

Favorite Memory _____

New Friends _____

Don't forget! _____

Date _____

At Sea ○   Port ○   _____

Weather ☀ ☁ ☂ ❄   Temperature _____

	Restaurant	Menu Choice
Breakfast		
Lunch		
Dinner		

Shipboard Activities

Excursions

Evening events _____

Attire _____

Favorite Memory _____

New Friends _____

Don't forget! _____

Date _____

At Sea ○   Port ○   _____

Weather ☀ ☁ ☂ ❄   Temperature _____

	Restaurant	Menu Choice
Breakfast		
Lunch		
Dinner		

Shipboard Activities   Excursions

Evening events _____

Attire _____

Favorite Memory _____

New Friends _____

Don't forget! _____

Date _____

At Sea ○   Port ○   _____

Weather ☀ ☁ ☂ ❄   Temperature _____

	Restaurant	Menu Choice
Breakfast		
Lunch		
Dinner		

Shipboard Activities

Excursions

Evening events _____

Attire _____

Favorite Memory _____

New Friends _____

Don't forget! _____

Date _____

At Sea ○   Port ○   _____

Weather ☀ ☁ ☂ ❄   Temperature _____

	Restaurant	Menu Choice
Breakfast		
Lunch		
Dinner		

Shipboard Activities

Excursions

Evening events _____

Attire _____

Favorite Memory _____

New Friends _____

Don't forget! _____

Date _____

At Sea ◯   Port ◯   _____

Weather ☀ ☁ ☂ ❄   Temperature _____

	Restaurant	Menu Choice
Breakfast		
Lunch		
Dinner		

Shipboard Activities

Excursions

Evening events _____

Attire _____

Favorite Memory _____

New Friends _____

Don't forget! _____

Date _____

At Sea ○   Port ○   _____

Weather ☀ ☁ ☂ ❄   Temperature _____

	Restaurant	Menu Choice
Breakfast		
Lunch		
Dinner		

Shipboard Activities   Excursions

Evening events _____

Attire _____

Favorite Memory _____

New Friends _____

Don't forget! _____

Date _____

At Sea ○   Port ○   _____

Weather ☀ ☁ ☂ ❄   Temperature _____

	Restaurant	Menu Choice
Breakfast		
Lunch		
Dinner		

Shipboard Activities

Excursions

Evening events _____

Attire _____

Favorite Memory _____

New Friends _____

Don't forget! _____

Date _____

At Sea ○   Port ○   _____

Weather ☀ ☁ ☂ ❄   Temperature _____

	Restaurant	Menu Choice
Breakfast		
Lunch		
Dinner		

Shipboard Activities   Excursions

Evening events _____

Attire _____

Favorite Memory _____

New Friends _____

Don't forget! _____

Date _____

At Sea ○   Port ○   _____

Weather ☀ ☁ ☂ ❄   Temperature _____

	Restaurant	Menu Choice
Breakfast		
Lunch		
Dinner		

Shipboard Activities

Excursions

Evening events _____

Attire _____

Favorite Memory _____

New Friends _____

Don't forget! _____

Date _____

At Sea ○   Port ○   _____

Weather ☀ ☁ ☂ ❄   Temperature _____

	Restaurant	Menu Choice
Breakfast		
Lunch		
Dinner		

Shipboard Activities

Excursions

Evening events _____

Attire _____

Favorite Memory _____

New Friends _____

Don't forget! _____

Date _____

At Sea ○   Port ○   _____

Weather ☀ ☁ ☂ ❄   Temperature _____

	Restaurant	Menu Choice
Breakfast		
Lunch		
Dinner		

Shipboard Activities

Excursions

Evening events _____

Attire _____

Favorite Memory _____

New Friends _____

Don't forget! _____

Date _____

At Sea ○   Port ○   _____

Weather ☀ ☁ ☂ ❄   Temperature _____

	Restaurant	Menu Choice
Breakfast		
Lunch		
Dinner		

Shipboard Activities   Excursions

Evening events _____

Attire _____

Favorite Memory _____

New Friends _____

Don't forget! _____

Date _____

At Sea ○ Port ○ _____

Weather ☀ ☁ ☂ ❄   Temperature _____

	Restaurant	Menu Choice
Breakfast		
Lunch		
Dinner		

Shipboard Activities

Excursions

Evening events _____

Attire _____

Favorite Memory _____

New Friends _____

Don't forget! _____

Date _____

At Sea ○   Port ○   _____

Weather ☀ ☁ ☂ ❄   Temperature _____

	Restaurant	Menu Choice
Breakfast		
Lunch		
Dinner		

Shipboard Activities   Excursions

Evening events _____

Attire _____

Favorite Memory _____

New Friends _____

Don't forget! _____

Date _____

At Sea ○   Port ○   _____

Weather ☀ ☁ ☂ ❄   Temperature _____

	Restaurant	Menu Choice
Breakfast		
Lunch		
Dinner		

Shipboard Activities

Excursions

Evening events _____

Attire _____

Favorite Memory _____

New Friends _____

Don't forget! _____

Date _____

At Sea ○   Port ○   _____

Weather ☀ ☁ ☂ ❄   Temperature _____

	Restaurant	Menu Choice
Breakfast		
Lunch		
Dinner		

Shipboard Activities

Excursions

Evening events _____

Attire _____

Favorite Memory _____

New Friends _____

Don't forget! _____

Date _____

At Sea ○   Port ○   _____

Weather ☀ ☁ ☂ ❄   Temperature _____

	Restaurant	Menu Choice
Breakfast		
Lunch		
Dinner		

Shipboard Activities

Excursions

Evening events _____

Attire _____

Favorite Memory _____

New Friends _____

Don't forget! _____

Date _____

At Sea ○   Port ○   _____

Weather ☀ ☁ ☂ ❄   Temperature _____

	Restaurant	Menu Choice
Breakfast		
Lunch		
Dinner		

Shipboard Activities

Excursions

Evening events _____

Attire _____

Favorite Memory _____

New Friends _____

Don't forget! _____

Date _____

At Sea ○   Port ○   _____

Weather ☀ ☁ ☂ ❄   Temperature _____

	Restaurant	Menu Choice
Breakfast		
Lunch		
Dinner		

Shipboard Activities

Excursions

Evening events _____

Attire _____

Favorite Memory _____

New Friends _____

Don't forget! _____

Date _____

At Sea ○   Port ○   _____

Weather ☀ ☁ ☂ ❄   Temperature _____

	Restaurant	Menu Choice
Breakfast		
Lunch		
Dinner		

Shipboard Activities

Excursions

Evening events _____

Attire _____

Favorite Memory _____

New Friends _____

Don't forget! _____

Date _____

At Sea ○   Port ○   _____

Weather ☀ ☁ ☂ ❄   Temperature _____

	Restaurant	Menu Choice
Breakfast		
Lunch		
Dinner		

Shipboard Activities

Excursions

Evening events _____

Attire _____

Favorite Memory _____

New Friends _____

Don't forget! _____

Date _____

At Sea ○   Port ○   _____

Weather ☀ ☁ ☂ ❄   Temperature _____

	Restaurant	Menu Choice
Breakfast		
Lunch		
Dinner		

Shipboard Activities

Excursions

Evening events _____

Attire _____

Favorite Memory _____

New Friends _____

Don't forget! _____

Date _____

At Sea ○   Port ○   _____

Weather ☀ ☁ ☂ ❄   Temperature _____

	Restaurant	Menu Choice
Breakfast		
Lunch		
Dinner		

Shipboard Activities

Excursions

Evening events _____

Attire _____

Favorite Memory _____

New Friends _____

Don't forget! _____

Date _____

At Sea ○ Port ○ _____

Weather ☀ ☁ ☂ ❄   Temperature _____

	Restaurant	Menu Choice
Breakfast		
Lunch		
Dinner		

Shipboard Activities

Excursions

Evening events _____

Attire _____

Favorite Memory _____

New Friends _____

Don't forget! _____

Date _____

At Sea ○   Port ○   _____

Weather ☀ ☁ ☂ ❄   Temperature _____

	Restaurant	Menu Choice
Breakfast		
Lunch		
Dinner		

Shipboard Activities

Excursions

Evening events _____

Attire _____

Favorite Memory _____

New Friends _____

Don't forget! _____

Date _____

At Sea ○   Port ○   _____

Weather ☀ ☁ ☂ ❄   Temperature _____

	Restaurant	Menu Choice
Breakfast		
Lunch		
Dinner		

Shipboard Activities

Excursions

Evening events _____

Attire _____

Favorite Memory _____

New Friends _____

Don't forget! _____

Date _____

At Sea ○   Port ○   _____

Weather ☀ ☁ ☂ ❄   Temperature _____

	Restaurant	Menu Choice
Breakfast		
Lunch		
Dinner		

Shipboard Activities

Excursions

Evening events _____

Attire _____

Favorite Memory _____

New Friends _____

Don't forget! _____

Date _____

At Sea ○   Port ○   _____

Weather ☀ ☁ ☂ ❄   Temperature _____

	Restaurant	Menu Choice
Breakfast		
Lunch		
Dinner		

Shipboard Activities

Excursions

Evening events _____

Attire _____

Favorite Memory _____

New Friends _____

Don't forget! _____

Date _____

At Sea ○   Port ○   _____

Weather ☀ ☁ ☂ ❄   Temperature _____

	Restaurant	Menu Choice
Breakfast		
Lunch		
Dinner		

Shipboard Activities

Excursions

Evening events _____

Attire _____

Favorite Memory _____

New Friends _____

Don't forget! _____

Date _____

At Sea ○   Port ○   _____

Weather ☀ ☁ ☂ ❄   Temperature _____

	Restaurant	Menu Choice
Breakfast		
Lunch		
Dinner		

Shipboard Activities

Excursions

Evening events _____

Attire _____

Favorite Memory _____

New Friends _____

Don't forget! _____

Date _____

At Sea ○   Port ○   _____

Weather ☀ ☁ ☂ ❄   Temperature _____

	Restaurant	Menu Choice
Breakfast		
Lunch		
Dinner		

Shipboard Activities

Excursions

Evening events _____

Attire _____

Favorite Memory _____

New Friends _____

Don't forget! _____

Date _____

At Sea ○   Port ○   _____

Weather ☀ ☁ ☂ ❄   Temperature _____

	Restaurant	Menu Choice
Breakfast		
Lunch		
Dinner		

Shipboard Activities

Excursions

Evening events _____

Attire _____

Favorite Memory _____

New Friends _____

Don't forget! _____

Date _____

At Sea ○   Port ○   _____

Weather ☀ ☁ ☂ ❄   Temperature _____

	Restaurant	Menu Choice
Breakfast		
Lunch		
Dinner		

Shipboard Activities

Excursions

Evening events _____

Attire _____

Favorite Memory _____

New Friends _____

Don't forget! _____

Date _____

At Sea ○   Port ○   _____

Weather ☀ ☁ ☂ ❄   Temperature _____

	Restaurant	Menu Choice
Breakfast		
Lunch		
Dinner		

Shipboard Activities

Excursions

Evening events _____

Attire _____

Favorite Memory _____

New Friends _____

Don't forget! _____

Date _____

At Sea ○   Port ○   _____

Weather ☀ ☁ ☂ ❄   Temperature _____

	Restaurant	Menu Choice
Breakfast		
Lunch		
Dinner		

Shipboard Activities

Excursions

Evening events _____

Attire _____

Favorite Memory _____

New Friends _____

Don't forget! _____

Date _____

At Sea ○   Port ○   _____

Weather ☀ ☁ ☂ ❄   Temperature _____

	Restaurant	Menu Choice
Breakfast		
Lunch		
Dinner		

Shipboard Activities

Excursions

Evening events _____

Attire _____

Favorite Memory _____

New Friends _____

Don't forget! _____

Date _____

At Sea ○   Port ○   _____

Weather ☀ ☁ ☂ ❄   Temperature _____

	Restaurant	Menu Choice
Breakfast		
Lunch		
Dinner		

Shipboard Activities

Excursions

Evening events _____

Attire _____

Favorite Memory _____

New Friends _____

Don't forget! _____

Date _____

At Sea ○   Port ○   _____

Weather ☀ ☁ ☂ ❄   Temperature _____

	Restaurant	Menu Choice
Breakfast		
Lunch		
Dinner		

Shipboard Activities   Excursions

Evening events _____

Attire _____

Favorite Memory _____

New Friends _____

Don't forget! _____

Date _____

At Sea ◯   Port ◯   _____

Weather ☀ ☁ ☂ ❄   Temperature _____

	Restaurant	Menu Choice
Breakfast		
Lunch		
Dinner		

Shipboard Activities

Excursions

Evening events _____

Attire _____

Favorite Memory _____

New Friends _____

Don't forget! _____

Date _____

At Sea ○   Port ○   _____

Weather ☀ ☁ ☂ ❄   Temperature _____

	Restaurant	Menu Choice
Breakfast		
Lunch		
Dinner		

Shipboard Activities

Excursions

Evening events _____

Attire _____

Favorite Memory _____

New Friends _____

Don't forget! _____

Date _____

At Sea ○   Port ○   _____

Weather ☀ ☁ ☂ ❄   Temperature _____

	Restaurant	Menu Choice
Breakfast		
Lunch		
Dinner		

Shipboard Activities

Excursions

Evening events _____

Attire _____

Favorite Memory _____

New Friends _____

Don't forget! _____

Date _____

At Sea ○   Port ○   _____

Weather ☀ ☁ ☂ ❄   Temperature _____

	Restaurant	Menu Choice
Breakfast		
Lunch		
Dinner		

Shipboard Activities

Excursions

Evening events _____

Attire _____

Favorite Memory _____

New Friends _____

Don't forget! _____

Date _____

At Sea ○   Port ○   _____

Weather ☀ ☁ ☂ ❄   Temperature _____

	Restaurant	Menu Choice
Breakfast		
Lunch		
Dinner		

Shipboard Activities

Excursions

Evening events _____

Attire _____

Favorite Memory _____

New Friends _____

Don't forget! _____

Date _____

At Sea ○   Port ○   _____

Weather ☀ ☁ ☂ ❄   Temperature _____

	Restaurant	Menu Choice
Breakfast		
Lunch		
Dinner		

Shipboard Activities

Excursions

Evening events _____

Attire _____

Favorite Memory _____

New Friends _____

Don't forget! _____

Date _____

At Sea ○   Port ○   _____

Weather ☀ ☁ ☂ ❄   Temperature _____

	Restaurant	Menu Choice
Breakfast		
Lunch		
Dinner		

Shipboard Activities

Excursions

Evening events _____

Attire _____

Favorite Memory _____

New Friends _____

Don't forget! _____

Date _____

At Sea ○   Port ○   _____

Weather ☀ ☁ ☂ ❄   Temperature _____

	Restaurant	Menu Choice
Breakfast		
Lunch		
Dinner		

Shipboard Activities

Excursions

Evening events _____

Attire _____

Favorite Memory _____

New Friends _____

Don't forget! _____

Date _____

At Sea ○   Port ○   _____

Weather ☀ ☁ ☂ ❄   Temperature _____

	Restaurant	Menu Choice
Breakfast		
Lunch		
Dinner		

Shipboard Activities

Excursions

Evening events _____

Attire _____

Favorite Memory _____

New Friends _____

Don't forget! _____

Date _____

At Sea ○   Port ○   _____

Weather ☀ ☁ ☂ ❄   Temperature _____

	Restaurant	Menu Choice
Breakfast		
Lunch		
Dinner		

Shipboard Activities   Excursions

Evening events _____

Attire _____

Favorite Memory _____

New Friends _____

Don't forget! _____

Date _____

At Sea ○   Port ○   _____

Weather ☀ ☁ ☂ ❄   Temperature _____

	Restaurant	Menu Choice
Breakfast		
Lunch		
Dinner		

Shipboard Activities

Excursions

Evening events _____

Attire _____

Favorite Memory _____

New Friends _____

Don't forget! _____

Date _____

At Sea ○   Port ○   _____

Weather ☀ ☁ ☂ ❄   Temperature _____

	Restaurant	Menu Choice
Breakfast		
Lunch		
Dinner		

Shipboard Activities

Excursions

Evening events _____

Attire _____

Favorite Memory _____

New Friends _____

Don't forget! _____

Date _____

At Sea ○   Port ○   _____

Weather ☀ ☁ ☂ ❄   Temperature _____

	Restaurant	Menu Choice
Breakfast		
Lunch		
Dinner		

Shipboard Activities

Excursions

Evening events _____

Attire _____

Favorite Memory _____

New Friends _____

Don't forget! _____

Date _____

At Sea ○   Port ○   _____

Weather ☀ ☁ ☂ ❄   Temperature _____

	Restaurant	Menu Choice
Breakfast		
Lunch		
Dinner		

Shipboard Activities   Excursions

Evening events _____

Attire _____

Favorite Memory _____

New Friends _____

Don't forget! _____

Date _____

At Sea ○   Port ○   _____

Weather ☀ ☁ ☂ ❄   Temperature _____

	Restaurant	Menu Choice
Breakfast		
Lunch		
Dinner		

Shipboard Activities

Excursions

Evening events _____

Attire _____

Favorite Memory _____

New Friends _____

Don't forget! _____

Date _____

At Sea ○   Port ○   _____

Weather ☀ ☁ ☂ ❄   Temperature _____

	Restaurant	Menu Choice
Breakfast		
Lunch		
Dinner		

Shipboard Activities

Excursions

Evening events _____

Attire _____

Favorite Memory _____

New Friends _____

Don't forget! _____

Date _____

At Sea ○   Port ○   _____

Weather ☀ ☁ ☂ ❄   Temperature _____

	Restaurant	Menu Choice
Breakfast		
Lunch		
Dinner		

Shipboard Activities

Excursions

Evening events _____

Attire _____

Favorite Memory _____

New Friends _____

Don't forget! _____

Date _____

At Sea ○   Port ○   _____

Weather ☀ ☁ ☂ ❄   Temperature _____

	Restaurant	Menu Choice
Breakfast		
Lunch		
Dinner		

Shipboard Activities

Excursions

Evening events _____

Attire _____

Favorite Memory _____

New Friends _____

Don't forget! _____

Date _____

At Sea ○ Port ○ _____

Weather ☀ ☁ ☂ ❄   Temperature _____

	Restaurant	Menu Choice
Breakfast		
Lunch		
Dinner		

Shipboard Activities

Excursions

Evening events _____

Attire _____

Favorite Memory _____

New Friends _____

Don't forget! _____

Date _____

At Sea ○   Port ○   _____

Weather ☀ ☁ ☂ ❄   Temperature _____

	Restaurant	Menu Choice
Breakfast		
Lunch		
Dinner		

Shipboard Activities   Excursions

Evening events _____

Attire _____

Favorite Memory _____

New Friends _____

Don't forget! _____

Date _____

At Sea ○   Port ○   _____

Weather ☀ ☁ ☂ ❄   Temperature _____

	Restaurant	Menu Choice
Breakfast		
Lunch		
Dinner		

Shipboard Activities

Excursions

Evening events _____

Attire _____

Favorite Memory _____

New Friends _____

Don't forget! _____

Date _____

At Sea ○   Port ○   _____

Weather ☀ ☁ ☂ ❄   Temperature _____

	Restaurant	Menu Choice
Breakfast		
Lunch		
Dinner		

Shipboard Activities   Excursions

Evening events _____

Attire _____

Favorite Memory _____

New Friends _____

Don't forget! _____

Date _____

At Sea ○   Port ○   _____

Weather ☀ ☁ ☂ ❄   Temperature _____

	Restaurant	Menu Choice
Breakfast		
Lunch		
Dinner		

Shipboard Activities

Excursions

Evening events _____

Attire _____

Favorite Memory _____

New Friends _____

Don't forget! _____

Date _____

At Sea ◯ Port ◯ _____

Weather ☀ ☁ ☂ ❄   Temperature _____

	Restaurant	Menu Choice
Breakfast		
Lunch		
Dinner		

Shipboard Activities   Excursions

Evening events _____

Attire _____

Favorite Memory _____

New Friends _____

Don't forget! _____

Date _____

At Sea ○　Port ○　_____

Weather　☀　☁　☂　❄　　　　　Temperature _____

	Restaurant	Menu Choice
Breakfast		
Lunch		
Dinner		

Shipboard Activities

Excursions

Evening events _____

Attire _____

Favorite Memory _____

New Friends _____

Don't forget! _____

Date _____

At Sea ○   Port ○   _____

Weather ☀ ☁ ☂ ❄   Temperature _____

	Restaurant	Menu Choice
Breakfast		
Lunch		
Dinner		

Shipboard Activities

Excursions

Evening events _____

Attire _____

Favorite Memory _____

New Friends _____

Don't forget! _____

Date _____

At Sea ○   Port ○   _____

Weather ☀ ☁ ☂ ❄   Temperature _____

	Restaurant	Menu Choice
Breakfast		
Lunch		
Dinner		

Shipboard Activities

Excursions

Evening events _____

Attire _____

Favorite Memory _____

New Friends _____

Don't forget! _____

Date _____

At Sea ○   Port ○   _____

Weather ☀ ☁ ☂ ❄   Temperature _____

	Restaurant	Menu Choice
Breakfast		
Lunch		
Dinner		

Shipboard Activities

Excursions

Evening events _____

Attire _____

Favorite Memory _____

New Friends _____

Don't forget! _____

Date _____

At Sea ○   Port ○   _____

Weather ☀ ☁ ☂ ❄   Temperature _____

	Restaurant	Menu Choice
Breakfast		
Lunch		
Dinner		

Shipboard Activities

Excursions

Evening events _____

Attire _____

Favorite Memory _____

New Friends _____

Don't forget! _____

Date _____

At Sea ○   Port ○   _____

Weather ☀ ☁ ☂ ❄   Temperature _____

	Restaurant	Menu Choice
Breakfast		
Lunch		
Dinner		

Shipboard Activities

Excursions

Evening events _____

Attire _____

Favorite Memory _____

New Friends _____

Don't forget! _____

Date _____

At Sea ○   Port ○   _____

Weather ☀ ☁ ☂ ❄   Temperature _____

	Restaurant	Menu Choice
Breakfast		
Lunch		
Dinner		

Shipboard Activities

Excursions

Evening events _____

Attire _____

Favorite Memory _____

New Friends _____

Don't forget! _____

Date _____

At Sea ○   Port ○   _____

Weather ☀ ☁ ☂ ❄   Temperature _____

	Restaurant	Menu Choice
Breakfast		
Lunch		
Dinner		

Shipboard Activities   Excursions

Evening events _____

Attire _____

Favorite Memory _____

New Friends _____

Don't forget! _____

Date _____

At Sea ○   Port ○   _____

Weather ☀ ☁ ☂ ❄   Temperature _____

	Restaurant	Menu Choice
Breakfast		
Lunch		
Dinner		

Shipboard Activities

Excursions

Evening events _____

Attire _____

Favorite Memory _____

New Friends _____

Don't forget! _____

Date _____

At Sea ○   Port ○   _____

Weather ☀ ☁ ☂ ❄   Temperature _____

	Restaurant	Menu Choice
Breakfast		
Lunch		
Dinner		

Shipboard Activities

Excursions

Evening events _____

Attire _____

Favorite Memory _____

New Friends _____

Don't forget! _____

Date _____

At Sea ○   Port ○   _____

Weather ☀ ☁ ☂ ❄   Temperature _____

	Restaurant	Menu Choice
Breakfast		
Lunch		
Dinner		

Shipboard Activities

Excursions

Evening events _____

Attire _____

Favorite Memory _____

New Friends _____

Don't forget! _____

Date _____

At Sea ○   Port ○   _____

Weather ☀ ☁ ☂ ❄   Temperature _____

	Restaurant	Menu Choice
Breakfast		
Lunch		
Dinner		

Shipboard Activities

Excursions

Evening events _____

Attire _____

Favorite Memory _____

New Friends _____

Don't forget! _____

Date _____

At Sea ○   Port ○   _____

Weather ☀ ☁ ☂ ❄   Temperature _____

	Restaurant	Menu Choice
Breakfast		
Lunch		
Dinner		

Shipboard Activities

Excursions

Evening events _____

Attire _____

Favorite Memory _____

New Friends _____

Don't forget! _____

Date _____

At Sea ◯   Port ◯   _____

Weather ☀ ☁ ☂ ❄   Temperature _____

	Restaurant	Menu Choice
Breakfast		
Lunch		
Dinner		

Shipboard Activities

Excursions

Evening events _____

Attire _____

Favorite Memory _____

New Friends _____

Don't forget! _____

Date _____

At Sea ○   Port ○   _____

Weather ☀ ☁ ☂ ❄   Temperature _____

	Restaurant	Menu Choice
Breakfast		
Lunch		
Dinner		

Shipboard Activities

Excursions

Evening events _____

Attire _____

Favorite Memory _____

New Friends _____

Don't forget! _____

Date _____

At Sea ○   Port ○   _____

Weather ☀ ☁ ☂ ❄   Temperature _____

	Restaurant	Menu Choice
Breakfast		
Lunch		
Dinner		

Shipboard Activities

Excursions

Evening events _____

Attire _____

Favorite Memory _____

New Friends _____

Don't forget! _____

Date _____

At Sea ○   Port ○   _____

Weather ☀ ☁ ☂ ❄   Temperature _____

	Restaurant	Menu Choice
Breakfast		
Lunch		
Dinner		

Shipboard Activities

Excursions

Evening events _____

Attire _____

Favorite Memory _____

New Friends _____

Don't forget! _____

Date _____

At Sea ○   Port ○   _____

Weather ☀ ☁ ☂ ❄   Temperature _____

	Restaurant	Menu Choice
Breakfast		
Lunch		
Dinner		

Shipboard Activities

Excursions

Evening events _____

Attire _____

Favorite Memory _____

New Friends _____

Don't forget! _____

Date _____

At Sea ○   Port ○   _____

Weather ☀ ☁ ☂ ❄   Temperature _____

	Restaurant	Menu Choice
Breakfast		
Lunch		
Dinner		

Shipboard Activities

Excursions

Evening events _____

Attire _____

Favorite Memory _____

New Friends _____

Don't forget! _____

Date _____

At Sea ○   Port ○   _____

Weather ☀ ☁ ☂ ❄   Temperature _____

	Restaurant	Menu Choice
Breakfast		
Lunch		
Dinner		

Shipboard Activities

Excursions

Evening events _____

Attire _____

Favorite Memory _____

New Friends _____

Don't forget! _____

Date _____

At Sea ○   Port ○   _____

Weather ☀ ☁ ☂ ❄   Temperature _____

	Restaurant	Menu Choice
Breakfast		
Lunch		
Dinner		

Shipboard Activities

Excursions

Evening events _____

Attire _____

Favorite Memory _____

New Friends _____

Don't forget! _____

Date _____

At Sea ○   Port ○   _____

Weather ☀ ☁ ☂ ❄   Temperature _____

	Restaurant	Menu Choice
Breakfast		
Lunch		
Dinner		

Shipboard Activities

Excursions

Evening events _____

Attire _____

Favorite Memory _____

New Friends _____

Don't forget! _____

Date _____

At Sea ○   Port ○   _____

Weather ☀ ☁ ☂ ❄   Temperature _____

	Restaurant	Menu Choice
Breakfast		
Lunch		
Dinner		

Shipboard Activities

Excursions

Evening events _____

Attire _____

Favorite Memory _____

New Friends _____

Don't forget! _____

Date _____

At Sea ○   Port ○   _____

Weather ☀ ☁ ☂ ❄   Temperature _____

	Restaurant	Menu Choice
Breakfast		
Lunch		
Dinner		

Shipboard Activities

Excursions

Evening events _____

Attire _____

Favorite Memory _____

New Friends _____

Don't forget! _____

Date _____

At Sea ○   Port ○   _____

Weather ☀ ☁ ☂ ❄   Temperature _____

	Restaurant	Menu Choice
Breakfast		
Lunch		
Dinner		

Shipboard Activities

Excursions

Evening events _____

Attire _____

Favorite Memory _____

New Friends _____

Don't forget! _____

Date _____

At Sea ◯   Port ◯   _____

Weather ☀ ☁ ☂ ❄   Temperature _____

	Restaurant	Menu Choice
Breakfast		
Lunch		
Dinner		

Shipboard Activities   Excursions

Evening events _____

Attire _____

Favorite Memory _____

New Friends _____

Don't forget! _____

www.ingramcontent.com/pod-product-compliance
Lightning Source LLC
Chambersburg PA
CBHW081233080526
44587CB00022B/3927